Tarantula Spiders

ABDO
Publishing Company

A Buddy Book
by
Julie Murray

VISIT US AT
www.abdopub.com

Published by Buddy Books, an imprint of ABDO Publishing Company, 4940 Viking Drive, Suite 622, Edina, Minnesota 55435. Copyright © 2003 by Abdo Consulting Group, Inc. International copyrights reserved in all countries. No part of this book may be reproduced in any form without written permission from the publisher.

Printed in the United States.

Edited by: Christy DeVillier
Contributing Editors: Matt Ray, Michael P. Goecke
Graphic Design: Maria Hosley
Image Research: Deborah Coldiron
Cover Photograph: Mark Kostich
Interior Photographs: Mark Kostich, Minden Pictures, Photodisc, Rick C. West

Library of Congress Cataloging-in-Publication Data

Murray, Julie, 1969-
  Tarantula spiders / Julie Murray.
     p. cm. — (Animal kingdom)
  Summary: An introduction to the physical characteristics, habitat, and behavior of tarantulas.
  ISBN 1-57765-729-2
     1. Tarantulas—Juvenile literature. [1. Tarantulas. 2. Spiders.] I. Title. II. Animal kingdom (Edina, Minn.)

QL458.42.T5 M85 2002
595.4'4—dc21

2001046439

Contents

Arachnids

There are more than 35,000 kinds of spiders. Spiders are not insects. They are **arachnids**. All arachnids have eight legs. Scorpions and ticks are arachnids, too.

Tarantulas are large and hairy spiders. There are more than 800 kinds of tarantulas. Some people keep tarantulas as pets. Chilean rose tarantulas make good pets.

Ticks, scorpions, and spiders are all arachnids.

Size And Color

Different tarantulas are different sizes. Many North American tarantulas grow to become two to four inches (5 to 10 cm) across. Thai tiger tarantulas can grow to become about six inches (15 cm) across. Goliath tarantulas can grow to become 10 inches (25 cm) across.

Cobalt blue tarantula

Tarantulas may be brown, black, red, or blue. A Chilean common tarantula is brown all over. Some tarantulas have striped legs like the Mexican red-kneed tarantula.

Eight Eyes
Tarantulas have eight eyes.

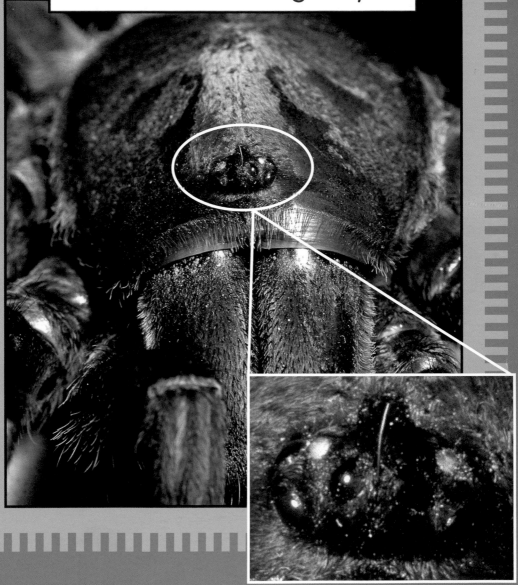

Body Parts

Like all spiders, tarantulas have two main body parts. The front part is the **cephalothorax**. The cephalothorax houses the brain, eyes, mouth, and stomach.

The spider's back part is called the **abdomen**. The tarantula's heart and lungs are inside its abdomen. On the tip of the abdomen are the spider's **spinnerets**. Silk thread comes from the spinnerets.

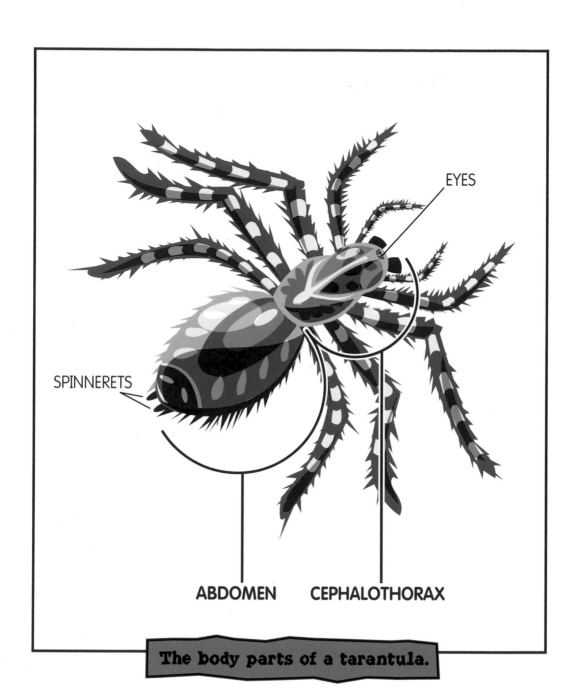

EYES

SPINNERETS

ABDOMEN   CEPHALOTHORAX

The body parts of a tarantula.

Where They Live

Different tarantulas live in different places around the world. Goliath tarantulas live in South America's jungles. Mexican blond tarantulas live in the desert. Many tarantulas live in holes in the ground called **burrows**. Other tarantulas live in trees.

This tarantula lives in Africa.

This tarantula lives in Central America.

13

Eating

Tarantulas are hunters. They eat crickets, grasshoppers, beetles, and other insects. Big tarantulas can catch lizards, frogs, snakes, and small birds.

Tarantulas grab their **prey** and bite it. A tarantula's bite poisons and kills its prey. Tarantulas may eat right away or save food for later.

Many tarantulas hunt at night.

Guarding Against Enemies

Birds, snakes, and other animals eat spiders. Tarantulas must guard themselves against these enemies. A tarantula's colors can help it hide from danger. Some tarantulas shed hair that can hurt enemies. Tarantulas can fight enemies by biting, too.

A tarantula with its front legs raised is ready to fight.

Tarantula Bites

Wild tarantulas are mostly shy. They often hide from people. A scared tarantula may bite someone. But most tarantula bites are harmless. They may feel like a bee sting.

Spiderlings

A female tarantula can lay 100 eggs at one time. She lays eggs in a special eggsac made of spider silk. A female tarantula guards her eggsac from danger.

Female tarantulas lay eggs in an eggsac made of spider silk.

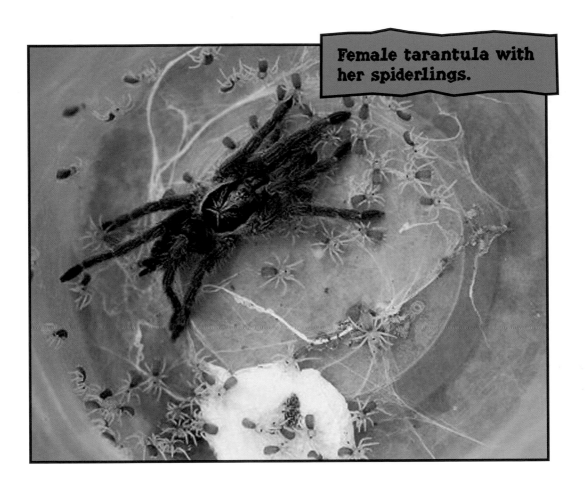

Female tarantula with her spiderlings.

Baby spiders are called spiderlings. Newly hatched tarantula spiderlings are light-colored. After a few weeks, they leave the eggsac. It takes years for tarantulas to become adults.

Important Words

abdomen the back end of a spider's body.

arachnid a small animal with two main body parts and eight legs.

burrow an animal's underground hole.

cephalothorax the front part of a spider's body.

prey any living thing that is killed and eaten by another.

spinnerets the part of a spider's body that makes silk.

Web Sites

Hays' Tarantula Web Pages

http://jrscience.wcp.muohio.edu/
html/tarantulas.html
This site has detailed information and pictures
of tarantulas.

Tarantulas.com

www.tarantulas.com
Discover how to keep tarantulas as pets.

Spider Facts

www.explorit.org/science/spider.html
Learn all about spiders at this web site.

Index

24